MEPHISTO WALTZ
and Other Works

for Solo Piano

FRANZ LISZT

DOVER PUBLICATIONS, INC., NEW YORK

Bibliographical Note

This Dover edition, first published in 1994, is a new compilation of works previously published in separate collections. Eleven works were originally published in *Franz Liszt, Klavierwerke* (Emil von Sauer, ed.) by C. F. Peters, Frankfurt, n.d. Works from Vol. V, *Original-Kompositionen I*, include: *Polonaise I, Polonaise II, Mephisto-Walzer I, Valse-Impromptu, Première Valse oubliée* and *Grand Galop chromatique*. Works from Vol. VI, *Original-Kompositionen II*, include *Liebesträume: Drei Notturnos*. Works from Vol. XII, *Supplement*, include: *Gretchen* and *Phantasie und Fuge über das Thema BACH*. The remaining six works in the Dover edition were originally published in unidentified editions, n.d.: *Czárdás Macabre, Nuages gris, La lugubre gondola I and II, Unstern!* and *Spanish Rhapsody*.

A unified, annotated list of contents has been added, titles given in the language most commonly associated with the music, and dates of composition and publication corrected where necessary. The Dover edition also includes the texts of the songs on which the *Liebesträume* are based, with new English translations by Stanley Appelbaum.

Library of Congress Cataloging-in-Publication Data

Liszt, Franz, 1811–1886.
    [Piano music. Selections]
    Mephisto waltz and other works for solo piano / Franz Liszt.
    p. of music.
    Reprint. "New compilation of works previously published in separate collections."
    Contents: Mephisto waltz : no. 1—Liebesträume : no. 1 in A-flat major ; no. 2 in E major ; no. 3 in A-flat major—Two polonaises : no. 1 in C minor ; no. 2 in E major—Fantasia and fugue on the theme BACH—Valse oubliée : no. 1—Unstern: Sinistre, disastro—Nuages gris—Grand galop chromatique—Valse-impromptu : in A-flat major—La lugubre gondola : I & II—Czárdás macabre—Gretchen : from A Faust symphony—Rhapsodie espagnole.
    ISBN 0-486-28147-7 (pbk.)
    1. Piano music.   I. Title.
M22.L77D6   1994   94-4562
                                                                          CIP
                                                                                      M

Manufactured in the United States of America
Dover Publications, Inc., 31 East 2nd Street, Mineola, N.Y. 11501

CONTENTS

[Titles are given in the language most commonly associated with the music.]

[Composed for orchestra, ca. 1860, as "The Dance in the Village Inn" ("Der Tanz in der Dorfschenke"), the second of *Two Episodes from Lenau's "Faust"*; Episode 1 is "The Ride by Night." The work draws its imagery from Nicholas Lenau's dramatic poem containing episodes omitted from Goethe's version of the Faust legend. Liszt's piano transcription, better known as *Mephisto Waltz No. 1*, was dedicated to Carl Tausig, the most famous of the first generation of Liszt pupils.]

[Piano transcriptions of three Liszt songs, published as a set in 1850: No. 1—*Hohe Liebe* (*Lofty Love*), ca. 1849; No. 2—*Seliger Tod* (*Blissful Death*), ca. 1849, also known by its first line of text: "Gestorben war ich" ("I had died"); No. 3—*O Lieb* (*Oh, Love*), ca. 1845. Full texts with English translations, p. 25.]

[Composed in 1851; published in 1852]

[Originally written for organ, in 1855, as *Prelude and Fugue on the Name BACH*. Revised, ca. 1870, and transcribed for piano under the alternate title *Fantasia and Fugue on the Theme BACH*.]

[The first of *Trois Valses Oubliées*, composed 1881–ca. 1885. A fourth waltz was discovered in the United States and published there in 1954.]

The following works were edited by Emil von Sauer:

Mephisto Waltz No. 1
Liebesträume Nos. 1, 2, 3
Polonaises Nos. 1, 2
Fantasia and Fugue on the Theme BACH
Valse Oubliée No. 1
Grand Galop Chromatique
Valse-Impromptu in A-flat Major
Gretchen
Rhapsodie Espagnole

Mephisto Waltz No. 1

("The Dance in the Village Inn":
Episode from Lenau's poem "Faust")

(ca. 1860)

*) Mit diesen Ziffern deutet Liszt die rhythmische Betonung an | *) *Par ces chiffres Liszt indique l'accentuation rythmique* | *) Liszt uses these figures to indicate the rhythmical accentuation

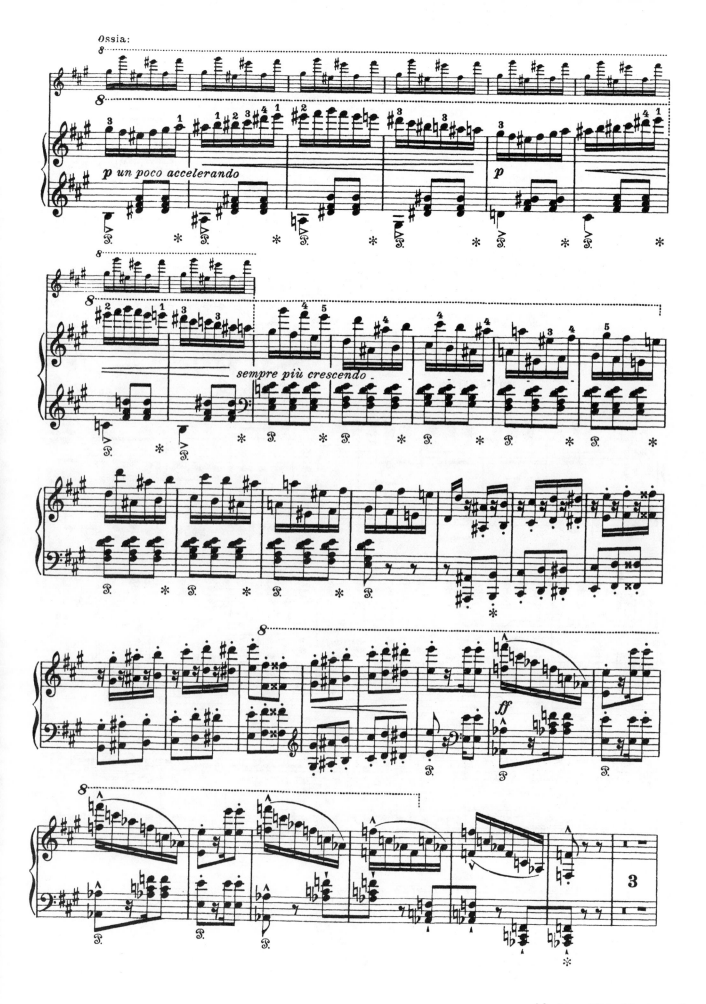

*) Ein hübscher Effekt ist, diesen Lauf
nur in der rechten Hand *glissando*, in
der Linken aber als *Skala* zu spielen.

*) *Il est d'un très bel effet d'exécuter ce
passage* glissando *de la main droite, et
en gamme de la main gauche.*

*) A fine effect is produced by playing
this run *glissando* with the right hand, the
left hand executing it as a *scale*.

Presto

LIEBESTRÄUME, 3 NOTTURNOS
(Dreams of Love, 3 Nocturnes)

Piano transcriptions of three Liszt songs on the following texts

English translations by Stanley Appelbaum

[LIEBESTRAUM NO. 1]

HOHE LIEBE
(Lofty Love)

Poem by Ludwig Uhland

In Liebesarmen ruht ihr trunken,
   Des Lebens Früchte winken euch;
Ein Blick nur ist auf mich gesunken,
   Doch bin ich vor euch allen reich.

Das Glück der Erde miss ich gerne
   Und blick, ein Märtyrer, hinan,
Denn über mir in goldner Ferne
   Hat sich der Himmel aufgetan.

You repose intoxicated in the arms of love,
   The fruits of life beckon to you;
Only one glance has fallen on me,
   But I am richer than all of you.

I gladly forgo earthly happiness
   And, as a martyr, I look upward,
For above me in the golden distance
   Heaven has opened.

[LIEBESTRAUM NO. 2]

SELIGER TOD
(Blissful Death)

Poem by Ludwig Uhland

Gestorben war ich
   Vor Leibeswonn,
Begraben lag ich
   In ihren Armen;

Erwecket ward ich
   Von ihren Küssen,
Den Himmel sah ich
   In ihren Augen.

I had died
   Of love's rapture,
I lay buried
   In her arms;

I was awakened
   By her kisses,
I saw Heaven
   In her eyes.

O LIEB
(Oh, Love)

Poem by Ferdinand Freiligrath

O lieb, o lieb so lang du lieben kannst, so
    lang du lieben magst.
  Die Stunde kommt, wo du an Gräbern
    stehst und klagst.
Und sorge dass dein Herze glüht, und Liebe
    hegt und Liebe trägt,
  So lang ihm noch ein ander Herz in Liebe
    warm entgegenschlägt.

Und wer dir seine Brust erschliesst, o tu ihm
    was du kannst zu lieb
  Und mach ihm jede Stunde froh, und
    mach ihm keine Stunde trüb!
Und hüte deine Zunge wohl: bald ist ein
    hartes Wort entflohn.
  O Gott—es war nicht bös gemeint—
  Der andre aber geht und weint.

Oh, love, oh love as long as you can love, as
    long as you wish to love.
  The hour will come when you stand by
    graves and lament.
And take care that your heart glows, and
    harbors love and bears love,
  As long as another heart still beats in
    return, warm with love.

And whoever uncovers your heart, oh, do all
    the lovable things for him you can,
  And make every hour happy for him, and
    make no hour dreary for him!
And watch your tongue carefully: a harsh
    word escapes all too quickly.
  Oh, God—it wasn't meant to be cruel—
  But the other walks away and weeps.

Liebestraum No. 1
in A-flat Major
(1850)

Liebestraum No. 2

in E Major

(1850)

Quasi Lento, abbandonandosi

Liebestraum No. 3

in A-flat Major

(1850)

poco cresc. ed agitato

Polonaise No. 1

in C Minor

(1851)

Polonaise No. 2
in E Major
(1851)

Fantasia and Fugue
on the Theme BACH
(ca. 1870)

Valse Oubliée No. 1

(1881)

Unstern: Sinistre, Disastro

(after 1880)

Nuages Gris

(1881)

To M^r le Comte Rodolphe d'Apponyi

Grand Galop Chromatique

(1838)

Valse-Impromptu
in A-Flat Major
(ca. 1850)

La Lugubre Gondola I

(1882)

La Lugubre Gondola II

(1882)

Czárdás Macabre

(1881–2)

Gretchen

(2nd "Character Picture" from *A Faust Symphony*)

(1874)

150 Gretchen (from *A Faust Symphony*)

152   Gretchen (from *A Faust Symphony*)

162 Gretchen (from *A Faust Symphony*)

Rhapsodie Espagnole

Folies d'Espagne et Jota Aragonesa

(ca. 1863)

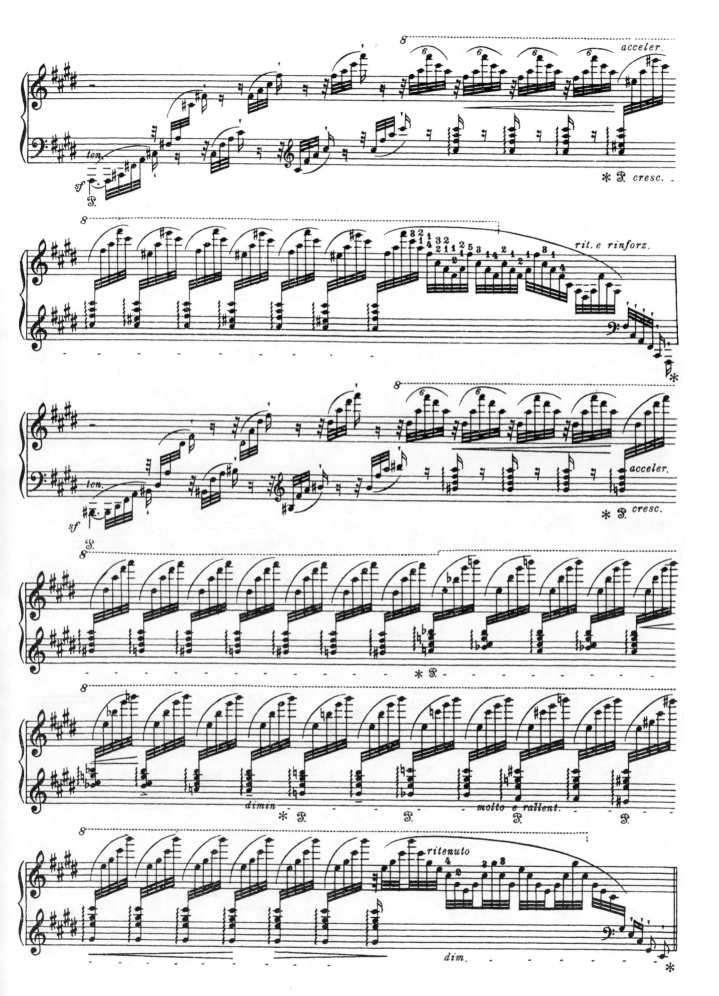

Non troppo allegro.